Nov 1992

~~7.50~~

4.00

Edward F. Jordan, jr.
Berkeley 1.22.87

# A FATHER AT A SOLDIER'S GRAVE

**by**

**FRITZ HAMILTON**

**Illustrations by Tom Hamilton**

DOWNTOWN POETS, NEW YORK

Cover design and photograph: Claire Cowdery

My thanks to David Gershator for his help in arranging and editing the fathers.



ISBN 0-917402-16-2

This publication is supported by publicly funded grants from the New York State Council on the Arts and the National Endowment for the Arts.

Published by
Downtown Poets Co-op
GPO Box 1720
Brooklyn, N.Y. 11202

**Produced at The Print Center, Inc., Box 1050, Brooklyn, N.Y., 11202, a non-profit printing facility for literary and arts-related publications. Funded by The New York State Council on the Arts and the National Endowment for the Arts.**

Previously published
*The Street and the Joint*
*The Plunge*
*Redman Is Redman's Mommy*
*Sores and Roses*

*To my father and Tommy . . . in memoriam*

I

The snow
Creeps quietly up your stone today
Your name and dates, my son
a powdered blur
The first freeze you have known
Across your death
There will be many more
They picked you up in pieces in a field
And sent you home
The sullenness of winter far
Beyond you now
I shall return to my car and
Turn on a football game
Rest assured, my son, next year
The snow will come again

## II

In 3 days it will be 1971
And you will embark on an adventure
You will have a full yr of being dead
And
Occasionally your daddy will visit you
And talk to you as if you were not
Last yr you were a soldier and in love
The yr before that a pretty fair sprinter
Not too long ago
A little guy listening to your daddy's stories and
Gobbling down your mother's cookies
But
In just 3 days it will be 1971
And I will embark on an adventure
Another yr of you being
Dead

## III

My boy
You never liked your old man much/sure
I gambled
But I did it for you and your mother
First it was the laundromats and
They failed
Then the hardware store
I didn't know enough about it
And the busline/hell
Not enough people in this town for a busline
Now
Nobody willing to lend me any more money
I drive the cab/still
If you'd only stayed home
We might have gotten something started together
But no
You had to hate me and run off to war
Now just see where it's got you

## IV

You, Jose, leader of the Latin Kings taking
No shit from nobody . . . you
Kill at least three Spanish Cobras I know . . . you
frightening everybody, even me, your papa . . . you
Feel nothing . . . knocking up little Juanita but
Her papa too scared to do nothing . . . then
You go to Nam and
When Sgt. O'Leary tell you to stand watch you
Tell him you don't take shit from nobody and
He blow your head off with his M-16 because
He Irish

## V

All right, Chucky, you
Always wanted to be a priest and
You made it . . . to serve as chaplain on
The front bolstering
The courage and spirits of our beleaguered boys
Time after time risking your life to
Keep the Lord close to their hearts and
So you took that frightened shell-shocked kid
Away from the fire/ off alone into
The jungle to calm and comfort him only
To be killed at last by sniper fire/ worthy
Of a Medal of Honor I'm sure if
They hadn't found your dead teeth clamped upon
His dead penis

## VI

Wilbur
Your paintings still hang all
Over the house, as I guess they always will, but
I can't get myself to look at them because
When I do
I see you at your easel painting them and
I hear the song you whistled, always
So happy when you worked and always
The same song

## VII

So
Being blind
I can picture you here as
Clearly now as before you made off for
That senseless war and
When I kneel down and touch
The frozen mound over you I
Cannot quite believe what I feel
Until
I ask you how you are and
All I hear is the soft wind mourning and
From far off on the highway
The fading rumble of
A truck

## VIII

So the boy says, Vern
I got a job to do
Off to Viet Nam he goes and
They get trapped on this hill
He's one of three that get away/ then
He's captured
All decapitated but him/ sneaks
Off in the jungle when they aren't looking
Lost
A week in a swamp/ gets
Wounded by a stray shell/ still
Gets back to a hospital and saved
Then
Out late and drunk in Saigon
Car runs off the road
Everybody killed/ still
The graves here look the same and
I wonder about the jobs we got to do

## IX

Now
That you are dead and in the ground I
Have figured the bill, my son/ you cost me
From birth through all your sicknesses and
Special schooling, not to mention the basics of
Food and shelter, somewhere
Close to $187,563.57 . . . all
Blown away on that hill in Nam (kind
of like investing in the Market in
1929)

## X

He never was much
Wrote poems as
His brothers played football
Never
Even cared to watch the games
Fell in love with
The high school tramp/ ran off with her
And lived in this filthy commune
Went to war but wouldn't
Carry a gun/ only
A damn stretcher/ then
We get this note
"Dad, I hate this war. 'Violence
is still the sire of all the world's values.'"/ hell
My boy never had the guts for violence
Still
I guess he has a right to lie out here
With all the others

## XI

Sure
I fought the Second Great War/ then
Damn near froze along the Yalu River in
The Great Police Action
And in both cases, be assured, I
Little Tom Edwards, never did more than I had to
Always as little as I could get away with
You bet
I saw brave men/ and lying there dead
They looked a hell of a lot like the cowards
Now, Tommy Jr.
I understand you caught a bullet in the back
You were your father's son

## XII

Look at them
All in a row
I couldn't tell my son from the others
But for his name on the Cross
This is the way they lived
This is the way they fought
Not as one and alone
But together/ a great machine
This is America
It's made us what we are
Not a lonely Jesus but
A whole team of them
And not even Vince Lombardi
Could have fielded better
By gosh
I'm not here to mourn a son
I'm here to praise them all
Bless the Lord

XIII

My son Phil was there when
Milton Lee Olive/ black man from Chicago/ threw
Himself on a grenade/ sacrificing
Himself for his men and
A Medal of Honor/ well
Two weeks later
Phil threw himself on a grenade but
The damn thing wouldn't go off and
He died of pneumonia in Saigon
Now
Olive has a statue honoring him in Chicago/ they
Even made a hit song about him
But
My son lies out here like a common soldier
I'll have to write the President about this

## XIV

It meant more to him/ being black
He said to me, Dad
I'm going to fight, and when it's over
Something will be proved/ well
He didn't have much time/ got his head
Blown off the first day in the field
But we have a nice letter from his sergeant
Telling us he served well
And he lies with his black brothers right close
To the fence
Where he can look over at his white buddies in
The *main* cemetery
So
I guess he proved something

XV

Dennis/ my boy/ my big boy now
I am so sorry
I left your mother when you were very young
I never gave you what you needed
Either physically or emotionally
But I cried, my son, I cried for you
And my own inadequacies
Please excuse me now
For I am left confused
It's so different
This cold gray stone
This frozen dirt

## XVI

I have not had a drink this morning, Rodney
I have done it for you, my number 4 son, despite
My shrieking brains and great depression
To tell you straight
That your mother, 2 sisters, 5 brothers
Are all fine/ are all well/ that
I continue to work the 70-hr-wk to keep
Them fine and well and
Even if I have been drinking since
They shipped you home
I have not had a drink this morning, Rodney
Still
I do not understand a town
That keeps its bars closed Sunday

## XVII

Well, my son, you
Always hated me and all your kin and
Damn near everybody else/ all
Through high school fighting and stealing, even
Swiping the family Buick for that lark down South and
Totaling it in Miami, and now
We have on our bed table
The picture of you smiling at your senior prom (the
Only time I ever saw you smile) and
Every time I look at it I
Get this rock of mourning in
My throat (that was the finest
Car I ever owned)

## XVIII

Well, my good boy, you
Join the bloody Marines because
Your Margo is sleeping with another man and
Promptly get your balls shot off in
The field . . . then
Raging mad you go home to show your Margo
But she doesn't care because she's still
Sleeping with the other man . . . so
You take your old shotgun and blow off your head and
Minus one head and two balls you end up in
A much more faithful box than Margo's . . . but
Last time I saw your Margo she told me (if
It makes you feel any better, son) that
She made a mistake about that other man

## XIX

Ralph
The sun sets in my eyes
Your Cross
A pleading hand upon
My boots/ please
Remove it from me now
Your frozen flesh beyond
The cold/ beyond
My agony of thought
Of Loss
Of never seeing, hearing, touching
You again/ beyond
The seeking and
The futile striving and
For what?
Please, Ralph, your hand
Remove it from me
Now

## XX

I stand here/ the dirt
So dark and hard upon my Burt/ the snow
A great white frame around him
And I'm comforted by knowing
That nobody cares
That the corner article on the front page of
Our town newspaper is now
Being used to kindle the fire and
Wrap the garbage
And I too
Have garbage that needs wrapping

## XXI

Well, son, it's one thing for you to
Step on a misplaced mine in basic training and
Get shipped home as pieces of meat in a plastic
Bag but
It's something else when I, Patrick O'Sullivan from
Centuries of Irish bar owners, inspect
The gory remains to find one hand twice as
Big as the other and one foot of
A nigger!

## XXII

Thomas
You always were a do-gooder so
Every chance you get you go into the villages with
Food and candy for the children . . . playing
With them and spreading American good will until
That 10-yr-old gook takes your Mars Bars, smiles, and
Rips that blade up your gut and
All you can do is pat his little Cong head and die
And I guess it's good you did, Thomas, because
When your buddies caught him and cut off his hands and
Hanged him in the center of the village
You probably would have got sick all over your
Bag of candy

## XXIII

Sam
Your mother is dying of cancer
I've learned to live with it but
I can't stand her shrieking and
It's already put me in debt/ to keep
The corpse running/ a good $7,000
And I can't say things are peachy on the farm
It costs more to feed the hogs
Than I get back at market and
If I eat one more bite of pork, Sam
I'm going to turn into a worm
I found your dog Luke the other day
Rotting beside the road where
Some damn car had knocked him
As for me, I'm fine
Nothing wrong at all
Now
If you'll just roll over
I might want to lie down and rest a bit

## XXIV

I recall your face, Darrell
In our second floor apartment window
The colored lights flashing around you
You were waiting for me to come home
That Christmas Eve
Your face
Was very round and very happy
You were 5-yrs-old
Strange
That I should recall that now
A cold wind blowing
Powdered snow above your frozen eyes
I'm sure you do not care

## XXV

It's very cold out here, my son
I can't stay long
You, on the other hand
Will be here awhile
I won't worry
You
Who never got less than A
Who captained the basketball team
Who got the biggest scholarship in the state
President of your fraternity
Who had more women – ha ha ha
Than your father ever knew
Have always weathered everything

## XXVI

Maurice
As the physics teacher at Oswald High
I shall tell you that
You have gone through a valuable learning experience
You have learned
That pieces of shrapnel traveling at high velocities
Penetrate a skull and scramble brains
You have learned
That such a disruption of a body's nature
Can cause excruciating pain for wks
To make you shriek and cry until
Needlessly you die and learn no more
What you never learned and never will
Is the anger
The suffering
The emptiness
Of your father now

## XXVII

Kurt Phillips should see you now
Dammit
You were always second string to him
His backup quarterback
7th man on the basketball team and
He was All-State
He was valedictorian/ you of course
Were number 2
Dammit
Now he quarterbacks the Illini
And what are you, my son
A piece of mangled flesh in a box
It will be yrs before
I live down this shame

## XXVIII

My son
Before you were born I drifted and
I didn't care but
Then you came and gave me reason
To work hard to
Give you all I never had and
I climbed from a simple doorman to
President of the realty firm that
Managed the highrise/ all
For you, my boy, and now
I'm well to do and you're out here
So
I lay this wreath upon you, the
Biggest money can buy, even
Bigger than the one I saw on
Jack Kennedy's grave/ all
Because of you, my boy
Thanks!

## XXIX

Well, Biffer
Life is short
For you a little shorter than most
But at least before you died
You tasted love/ little Mary Mayfair
Queen of the junior prom/ daughter
Of rich insurance man Milt Mayfair/ and
You were married before
You went off to get killed/ and
Perhaps you were lucky, Biffer, for
You never got to learn about your Mary and
Big Derrick Hart/ and
You never got to hear him brag about it at
The Whitewater Saloon

## XXX

Shit, Zeke
You think you had it bad
You ain't never been to Korea
Got so cold out there
The feet froze off and
Always at night in them trenches
The little Reds'd come upon you, Zeke
Waves and waves of 'em
Too dark to see
They'd go right over you
And pretty soon it'd be over
Half our trench dead or moanin'
Dead Reds freezin' all around you
Shit, Zeke
All you was doin' was
Swabbin' up a Saigon mess hall when
The bomb came through your window

## XXXI

Son
When I was 17 my first and finest love
Ran off with the high school tuba player and
When I was 22 my fiancee ran off
To Africa to teach and marry a nigger prince
At 27
The woman I knocked up
Stuck me with child support and married a mailman
Then
I met your mother/ we had you/ happy
For 20 yrs until I caught her in the backyard hammock
Fucking my law partner
And now it's you who've left me
You
Who lie beneath the frozen dirt
And they
Everyone of them/ happy with someone
Happy and alive with someone

## XXXII

Hey, David
You recall how I told you
Of getting up early last summer and
Seeing the sun rise over Lake Michigan
Its red finger pointing at me
Washing at my feet
And how I screamed
How I was everything just then
Everything in me immense and beautiful
Well
How would you like to go to the lake with me
How about tomorrow morning, David
We'll see the sun rise together

## XXXIII

I brought your dog Ben to see you, Bob
You should see him sniffing at your feet and
Wagging his big red tail
He'll never forget your smell, Bob
Even now/ all covered with dirt and snow
Beautiful old Ben, he loves you, Bob
He's up around your face now/ all bent over
I think he''s going to cry
Oh no!
Oh no, Ben!
Not on his face!
Not on your master's face!

## XXXIV

Strange
After 8 yrs at Joliet
Bum rapped for grand larceny
Neither you nor your mother
Ever visiting/ ever writing
To come here now and
See your grave
The last time I saw you/ you
Were 11-yrs-old/ not quite
4 ft tall
How big you must have grown
To have a grave so large

## XXXV

You know what amazes me, boy?
After
You got blown up by that booby trap and
They sent you home in pieces, that
Old Mickey Mouse watch I bought you for your
16th birthday was . . . unlike yourself . . . still
Running

## XXXVI

Douglas
Since you let your sergeant shoot you
Your mother has gone crazy
Nothing that was yours/ both
Inside and outside the house/ can be touched
Your bed remains unmade as always/ the sheets
Still spotted from your healthy genitals/ dust
Has buried your baseball glove in
The corner of the room and your jockstrap
In the middle of the floor
The *Popular Mechanics* on your desk
Is still open to the broken down Ford/ worse yet
Your own broken down Ford rests
In the center of the backyard gathering rust with
The tools strewn around it/ one of your wrenches
Broke the blade of my lawnmower but
Your mother still
Won't let me pick any of that crap up
But I don't care any more because
I have moved to the cheap dirty Ace Hotel collecting
The love of bedbugs and
Negotiating with a lawyer to divorce your mother
The grounds for which you have so kindly provided
So Douglas
Even though your death at the hands of your sergeant
Was a disgrace
It was not without redeeming value

## XXXVII

Louis
I never told you this but I
Have murdered 2 people
First
When I was very young and hunting
I saw
A little girl wading in a stream
I think the bullet struck her head
I didn't check it out
Later you recall
I ran over Sid Miller with the truck
It was no accident, Louis
I could have stopped
And now I stand over you/ killed at war
And I feel just like I did after the girl and Sid
Absolutely nothing

## XXXVIII

Your Linda is as big as an oil drum, Joe
Congratulations
Next wk you'll be a father
And if it's a boy, it's Joe Jr.
If it's a girl, we'll call her Jo
Yes, my young soldier, you
Will be preserved in name and
Never forgotten
Not like some of the boys here
All looking alike in rows of Crosses/ why
I bet that 15th Cross along row 7
Is already forgotten
I just have a feeling

## XXXIX

Son
You know that $50,000 your late mother
Willed you
Well
It's all in the hands of your father now
Sleep well, sucker

## XL

Jim
I know why you sent your men to take that hill
You wanted the Silver Star
Just
Like I sent my men across the river in Korea
Now
I have the Silver Star and you
Having lost 60% of your men
Were murdered that night in your tent
Our price for glory

## XLI

Everybody said you looked like your mother
If people didn't know you at 19, she at 37
They'd think you brother and sister/ even
Lovers
She looked so young beside you/ then
She fell off the horse and you
Got your legs blown off in Cambodia to die
In a hospital over there and now
You lie here and she lies beside you
I guess it's only right
Now I'll go home and straighten up the house and
Fix my dinner

## XLII

Now what do I do
I'm 62-yrs-old and
My back ain't much good no more
Can't make enough to keep myself goin' sometimes
And him/ always a good boy
Always done what he's supposed to
Now
What about his Marge and the 4 babies
Well
At least he ain't around to see
What's gonna happen to 'em

## XLIII

My boy
You took your opium and
Went out stoned to kill
You
Slaughtered gooks in the swamp
Killed them on the hill
Murdered women and children in a ditch
All the time stoned
Then they sent you back unscratched to
Shoot heroin into your arm and die
A common bum
You're lucky we'll take you back to lie
In our American national cemetery

## XLIV

All this violence to
Make you a man . . . you
Going into Chicago with your friends to
Beat up homosexuals . . . then you
Kicking shit out of Tommy Schmidt and
Taking his girl . . . and
Fighting after every football game . . . and
Getting stomped out and almost killed after
That silly dance . ... . and
Now lying here, a victim of pneumonia while
Carousing through Saigon (what
Kind of pansy shit is
That?)

## XLV

My darling boy
You always went your way
You
Did nothing in school but knock up a cheerleader
You
Stole $500 from my cash register and
Blew it in Miami
When
It came to college
You spent the tuition money on a new car and
When
Your mother died
You went bowling/ fuck the funeral
Now
You're dead
I cannot stop these tears

## XLVI

You
Were the finest high school halfback in
The state until you got that knee injury and
Never played again . . . then
You were straight A's at Princeton before
Leading that protest and getting yourself
Thrown out . . . then
You were making more money than any lst yr
Insurance salesman in the history of your
Company before the breakdown and the
Hospitalization . . . and now
They tell me you shot down ten commies single
Handed to free the bridge before
Tripping and falling on your own
Bayonet . . . why, son, were you always such
A fuckup?

## XLVII

Looking
Out over the field this year, boy, I
Watched the drought kill off most the crop and
That damn fungus getting the rest and
Now
I'm looking over you covered with dirt
And maybe that's better than you coming
Home to find out what's happened because
Your ma's finally made it into the madhouse and
Your sister got knocked up by some damn
Hitchhiker she never saw again and
Your brother got his legs cut off at the factory
So
I reckon the good Lord's telling me something and
I reckon I'd best get down on my knees and
Thank Him cause
Tomorrow could be worse

## XLVIII

Richard
I trained you from infancy
To walk the high wire like your daddy and
Indeed you did
From the time you were five thrilling
Thousands beneath the big top
And
Then you go to Nam to step on a mine and
Get your pieces sent back in a plastic bag
Son
How many times did I tell you
To watch your step

## XLIX

My big boy
When you were born you
Gave us no peace
How many months I walked you
Every night to keep you settled
And when
The doctors said you had a brain dysfunction
We waited
Through your frustrations/ your tantrums
To outgrow it
Then
Your sophomore yr/ smallest
Boy in the school
I saw you become State wrestling champ and then
You grew
Strong/ tough/ intelligent
Not every father gets to see
It wasted in this way

L

Teddy, my son, they
Tell me you ran dope in Saigon keeping
Our American boys high and happy while
Making the best damn fighting team in
The world a bunch of sniveling junkies . . . until
That private from Iowa you hooked went crazy and
Blew you away in the canteen with an M-16 and
I guess I now know how that $235,000 got stuffed
In the lining of your coat the Marines sent
Back to us and
I don't care what they say, your daddy
Loves you

## LI

Well, Bart, you
Leaving your Vietnamese wife in our
House while you go back to Nam to get yourself
Killed . . . now
You know how hard it is to keep a yellow girl in
Oakton . . . you know how our neighbors fear and
Hate her like all them other boat people . . . with
Her hardly able to speak English and
Stinking up our house with her yellow smell . . . so
Now you ain't alive to protect her and (because
We love you) we're gonna keep your son but
Her we're gonna send back home to
The gooks

## LII

Thomas
Marge was over almost every day
Asking about you and
I'd try to keep her happy
Taking her to dinner
To a club or movie
I bought her presents and
Counseled her
I did it for you, Thomas
And
When we learned of your death
She cried in my arms
She doesn't come back any more
I guess I'll have to get my balls off elsewhere

## LIII

Gary
While you have been away
Your father has been getting rich
Producing parts for tanks
Now
I know it's hell on you boys, but dammit
You should be proud
You're doing a lot for the rest of us

## LIV

Son
You crazy bastard
I told you in Little League how
To hit the ball/ you never could
I showed you how to do the algebra problems
You flunked
I showed you how to cross body block
You
Blocked with a leg and got it smashed
Godamit, son
You fucked up in everything/ then
I told you to volunteer for Vietnam and
You did
Now
Look at you, you crazy sonofabitch
Why
Did you listen to your daddy

## LV

Sandy boy
I might not have another
Chance to tell you . . . your mother
As long as I've know her has always
Fucked everything in sight and
If you've ever questioned why
You look so little like your daddy, this
Might offer you an answer (not
The sweetest information to feed you but
I think you've reached a point where
You can handle it)

## LVI

My son/ my only son
The gates are shut
Upon your daddy now
The snow swirls over you
Beneath the moon and
Numbs my feet
I should have left you but
I do not care
Your mother
Brother Ed
Your baby sister Joan
And all the rest
Are gone from you as
You are gone from them
Soon
The night will end but
Not for you and
Not for me
The gates are shut upon
Your daddy now

## LVII

My son is dead
I can't say more